NÜRNBERG

Experience Nuremberg

Above: The large coat-of-arms (on the Tiergärt-ner Tower Gate) portrays an eagle with the youthful, long-haired head of a king.

Contents

BERG

Above: Schedel's Chronicle of the World depicted Nuremberg in around 1500. This view became the model for the ideal medieval city.

Photography: Elmar Hahn
Text: Walter Grzesiek
English: Terence Zuber
Layout: Klaus Schinagl

elmar hahn verlag

Nuremberg's Old Town – a History Book Comes to Life

Experience Nuremberg? Where would you like to start? Ask a local and he will mention his favorite yearly festivals while the history buff will recommend starting with the golden age of the former Free Imperial City. The economist will speak of an economic factor that sustains a population of two and one half million people and places the city among the top ten hi-tech centers in Germany. The tourist may reflect on the history and art in the medieval Kaiserburg Fortress, in the Gothic churches or in the neighboring Franconian Switzerland region. But everyone will agree on two typically Nuremberg specialties: the tiny bratwurst and the tasty Lebkuchen gingerbread.

This book's intent is to point out the variety of charming sights in and the uniqueness of the Old Town. Nuremberg would look entirely different if its inhabitants had modernized everything at the beginning of the industrial age. The five kilometer long prestigious medieval wall that proudly rises to eight meters in height in spots was to be torn down to make it easier on the flow of traffic as was the case in both Vienna and Paris. Fortunately, the cultural and historical significance of this massive fortified ring won the hearts of its citizens and the wall was maintained. Damage during the Second World War is hard to discern and 65 of the original 150 medieval towers are in place and now serve as pubs, youth centers or ateliers. No other European city can boast of such an accomplishment.

Medieval walls, the Fortress, the Old Town Hall as well as St. Sebald's and Our Lady's churches give testimony to Nuremberg's rise to a Free Imperial City in the 14th century. In his Golden Bull, in 1356, Emperor Charles IV decreed that in addition to Frankfurt, where the election of the king was held, and Aachen, where the king was crowned, Nuremberg would be the Free Imperial City in which the first day of the Imperial Diet was held. As of 1424 the Imperial Crown Jewels were kept in Nuremberg. The Golden Bull went a step further and ensured that the trade routes of the Holy Roman Empire passed through Nuremberg on their eastward

Left: Albrecht Dürer painted this idealistic portray of Emperor Charlemagne (768-814) with his Imperial sword, crown and orb on linden wood in 1511 (German National Museum). As of 1524 the Crown Jewels were exhibited annually on the Market Square.

Right: A self-portrait of Albrecht Dürer in 1500 at the age of 28. It hangs in the Old Pinakothek in Munich.

1500

Albertus Dürerus Noricus
ipsum me proprijs sic effin=
gebam coloribus aetatis
anno XXVIII

path; Nuremberg's merchants were thus predestined to financial success. These merchants also profited from the inventiveness of Nuremberg's craftsmen whose renown was worldwide.

A European Metropolis

Nuremberg's airport is a good example of the city's economic expansion to Eastern Europe after the Berlin Wall came down at the end of the eighties. New perspective markets began developing even when many a Franconian was not fully aware of this progress. For numerous years, passengers boarded at the local airport in order to get to a major hub such as Munich or Frankfurt; in the meantime, Nuremberg's airport has been turned into a hub with over 500 flights a week and 60 nonstop flights, many of them to Eastern European destinations. At the same time, the Rhine-Main-Danube Canal at the port is being transformed into a transcontinental water-rail-road center. The autobahn as well serves as a bridgehead to the east.

The European Union has designated greater Nuremberg officially as a metropolitan region and again, it takes time for some Franconians to display the necessary self-confidence in their own good fortune. The past decades weren't always as rosy and time and again, global markets put a damper on many a traditional manufactured product. Fortunately, the services and communications industries were and continue to exert their influence and new sectors have been thriving nicely. The MP3 player was invented in Erlangen, a neighboring city that due to its innovative technology has earned the title of "Bavarian State Medical Capital." Siemens, Adidas, Puma, INA- Schaeffler and Playmobil are the more prominent global companies that are located in the

vicinity of Nuremberg. The call center provider Sellbytel has created innumerable new positions. Nuremberg installed the first totally automatic driverless metro line in the world. Datev provides services for tax consultants and international certified accountants. The Society for Consumer Research (GfK) is a German company that

has earned international recognition. And not to be forgotten, Nuremberg is one of the top ten European trade fair locations and among the top fifteen worldwide.

The Eagle and the ICE

The role industrialization played in the city is on display in two technological museums: the German Rail Museum behind the Opera House and to the east of the Old Town, the Museum for

Above left: A wooden replica of the 19th century Old Town is on display in the City Museum in the Fembo House.

Above: Behaim's Globe dating back to 1494 (German National Museum) portrays a view of the world prior to America's discovery.

Left: A fountain at Heffner Square is dedicated to the clockmaker, Peter Henlein, who died in 1542.

Industrial Culture. The 170-year old history of trains in Germany can be carefully scrutinized in the DB rail museum – everything from a copy of Germany's first train, the Adler or Eagle, which ran between Nuremberg and Fürth as of 1835, to the sleek ICE 3 of the 21st century. Tracks leading to every point on the compass were built almost immediately after the success of the first rail route. The train station in the southern part of the city became the switchyard and was build in the middle of the Imperial Forest. Large enterprises such as MAN and Siemens settled nearby. The workforce came from the Upper Palatinate and soon workers' settlements and cooperatives mushroomed. In the year 2000 after the incorporation of several outlying communities, Nuremberg had a population of 260,000 or three times the number of inhabitants of 1875.

The Museum of Industrial Culture is housed in the former ironworks factory in Äusseren Sulzbacher Strasse. Technology buffs can study steam engines, printing presses, a motorcycle collection and fire engines and equipment. In addition, the museum features the 19th cen-

Above: The Eagle, Germany's first train, left Nuremberg for Fürth on December 7, 1835.

Right: The Transportation Museum covers a wide range of artifacts – everything from the 1835 Adler to the ICE 3 of the future.

tury way of life of all the social classes in Nuremberg. The museumgoer will be introduced to day-to-day routines and living and working conditions as well as art and culture, leisure activities and educational opportunities.

Culture and Commerce

What about the city in the 21st century? The Old Town with its superb medieval setting holds poetry readings, flee markets, late evening hours at the museums, Old Town fests, a Christmas Market and wine and asparagus festivals throughout the year. Nuremberg is a subtle blend of culture and commerce and because its inhabitants do live and shop in the city, it remains a lovely and lively place to explore. Although the city had to be almost entirely reconstructed to its medieval style after World War II, the arduous project was an architectural success and at the same time, made it possible to experience the narrow streets and close quarters of city life in the Middle Ages. Nuremberg is a proud city that looks to its future as a cosmopolitan center of economic growth offering quality of life conditions to its inhabitants.

Above: The oldest view of Nuremberg can be found on an altar in St. Lorenz's. Jodokus Krell painted it in 1483.

950 Years of Nuremberg

1050	Emperor Heinrich III frees Sigena, the wife of a civil servant, from bondage and permits her to become a citizen. This is the first documentation of the city.
1219	On November 8, as proof of his "special favor and fondness," Frederick II (1194-1250) grants the city sovereignty. The city has its own judicial system and begins collecting taxes.
1348	Craftsmen revolt against the patricians by taking over the city's coffers and government. One year later, Charles IV (1316-1378) reinstates the councilmen and has the rebels punished.
1356	At the Imperial Diet, Charles IV decrees in the Golden Bull that every Emperor has to hold the first day of his Imperial Diet in Nuremberg.
1390	Ulman Stromer runs the first German paper mill.
1424	The Imperial Crown Jewels arrive in Nuremberg.
1427	Nuremberg purchases the burgrave's property and he leaves the city.
1493	Hartmann Schedel (1440-1514) prints his Chronicle of the World on Anton Koberger's printing press.
1494	Martin Behaim makes the world's oldest existing globe.
1500	Nuremberg in its heyday counts 50,000 inhabitants.

1512	At the Imperial Diet, Emperor Maximilian commissions Albrecht Dürer (1471-1528) to carry out numerous projects.
1525	The city council meets in the Town Hall and Nuremberg becomes Protestant.
1635	During the Thirty Years' War, Nuremberg is able to conclude a separate peace agreement which costs the city 7.5 million guilders.
1793	Ludwig Tieck and Heinrich Wackenroder, two budding Romanticists, discover Nuremberg.
1806	Napoleon turns the city over to Bavaria. Nuremberg has a population of a mere 25,000 and is deep in debt. A lack of finances results in the sale of works of art and public buildings.
1835	Germany's first steam-operated train, the Adler or Eagle, travels between Nuremberg and Fürth.
1850	For the first time since 1499, Jews are permitted to reside in the city; the population reaches 50,000.
1900	Nuremberg has a population of 260,000 due to rapidly-growing industrialization and the incorporation of numerous surrounding towns and villages. The manufacture of vehicles, bicycles, pencils and electrical products as well as the hops trade puts Nuremberg on the global map.
1922	Julius Streicher, later known as the Franconian Führer, establishes the Nazi Party in Nuremberg.
1927	The Nuremberg Soccer Club wins the German championship for the fifth time since the end of WWI.
1933	Nuremberg becomes the venue for the Nazi Party rallies.
1934	At the German Reichstag, Herman Göring lays down the Nuremberg Laws which reduce Jews to second class citizens.
As of 1941	deportation of Nuremberg's Jewish population; 1,631 are sent to extermination camps and only 72 survive.
1945	On January 2, Allied Forces conduct their heaviest air attacks on the city. The majority of the Old Town is destroyed and 1,829 people lose their lives.
As of 1945	the Nuremberg Trials begin followed by twelve further trials.
1950	Nuremberg holds the first International Toy Fair.
1971	During Dürer's 500th anniversary celebration, Nuremberg presents itself as a culturally-active cosmopolitan city.
1995	The first International Human Rights Award is presented to Nuremberg.
2000	The city celebrates its 950th anniversary.
2005	The metropolis of Nuremberg becomes a European metropolitan region.
2006	World Cup Soccer games take place in Nuremberg.

View of the Old Town in 1945: the ruins of Our Lady's Church behind the Beautiful Fountain which survived because it had been encased.

The Rise of the City under the Protection of the Emperors

The best view of the Old Town is from the Fortress. German emperors often sojourned here for extended periods of time. They played an important role in the city's rise to one of the most influential medieval European cities. Skilled craftsmen, merchants and proud councilmen made Nuremberg famous.

A Medieval Metropolis

Whether travelers approach the Kaiserburg Fortress from the rear in a tour bus or climb the steep cobblestone path from the front, at some point, visitors will reach the fortress courtyard and gaze over the red roofs and gables of the Old Town just as kings and emperors gazed at their Free Imperial City hundreds of years ago.

From atop the Fortress, it is easy to imagine what the city was like in the Middle Ages. Although the majority of the buildings within the city wall are reconstructions following World War II, they stand where their predecessors stood and the street patterns remain unchanged. Down narrow lanes, slender buildings no higher than five stories nestle against one

another while their red slate roofs provide the backdrop for the green-roofed spires of St. Sebald's and St. Lorenz's as well as for the towers of Our Lady's Church and the Town Hall.

On the Market Square below, German rulers once presented the townspeople with the jewels of the Empire: the crown and scepter, the sword and Imperial orb. Prominent inhabitants included the cosmopolitan architect, Martin Behaim, the Humanist, Willibald Pirckheimer, and

the poet and shoemaker, Hans Sachs. The painter and craftsman, Albrecht Dürer, lived in one of the winding, narrow streets below the Kaiserburg. There are numerous spots in the Old Town that still bear witness to Nuremberg's blossoming period: the Pegnitz River whose riverbanks and bridges Dürer once set to canvas, the Town Hall where the councilmen administered justice and sent the convicted to the dungeons below, and the narrow half-timbered buildings below the Fortress in Tanner's Lane where the pipe-fitters, needle, marionette and music-chord makers dwelled. "Nuremberg wit" or inventiveness became the city's trademark. The patricians, councilmen and merchants all shared a common interest in the export of jewelry and silver products, armor and edged weapons as well as compasses and drawing compasses.

The pocket watch, thimble, vise and clarinet along with numerous other inventions help justify Nuremberg's widespread fame during the Middle Ages. The adage

Previous page: The Kaiserburg Fortress from the south at dusk; Heathen Tower is on the left and Sinwell Tower stands in the middle.

Left: The Fortress from the Pentagonal Tower; Sinwell Tower is on the left and Heathen Tower and the palace are in the background.

Above: The Kaiserburg covered in snow as seen from the north.

went: "If I had Venice's power, Augsburg's splendor, Nuremberg's wit, Strasbourg's heavy artillery and Ulm's wealth, I would be the wealthiest man in the world."

Looking from the Fortress beyond the medieval city walls, the visitor can easily imagine just what Nuremberg wit entails: there is an insurance company's administrative tower, the skyscrapers that house the federal employment offices, the ever-expanding fairgrounds and the telephone tower known among the locals as the "Nuremberg Egg" due to the oval clocks that adorn it. This is proof enough that the city is alive and healthy and future-oriented. Ever since machine manufacturing and the electric appliance industry left the city, the tourist industry and communications technologies as well as the services sector have gained in importance.

Whenever the CEOs of these future-oriented companies convene in the city and whenever high-ranking members of culture and politics want to celebrate, they gather in the same spot that Ger-

man kings and emperors received their princes and subjects: at the Fortress.

Protruding Cliff

The sandstone cliff (Old High German: nuorin) measuring 250 meters in length and 50 meters high has been looming above its wooded, marshy surroundings for over a thousand years and gave the early settlement beneath the rocky outcrop its name: Nuorin-berg, in English, Nuremberg. St. Sebald, a Salian settlement, was the first settlement in the city and in the 12th century, the Hohenstaufen settled south of the Pegnitz River in the St. Lorenz quarter. The Jewish quarter on the banks of the river between the two settlements was totally destroyed during a pogrom in 1349. The Heubrücke or Hay Bridge to the east and the Hangman's Footbridge to the west connected both quarters for the first time as of 1320. The city walls, which are still completely intact, were begun in 1346.

Above: The snow-covered path leading up to the Kaiserburg Fortress.

17

The Salian king, Heinrich III, chose the city as a military stronghold and on July 16, 1050, he bestowed upon "Norenberc" a signed certificate, in which he freed Sigena, the wife of a civil servant, from bondage and permitted her to become a citizen and follow a trade. Nuremberg's beginnings, therefore, were not marked by a military act or power politics, but rather, an act of liberation. The awarding of these rights enabled the city to rise to a Free Imperial City.

It was also Heinrich III who entrusted the city with the right to hold markets, coin money and collect customs. Surrounded by dense forests, a military stronghold was set up along the east-west trade route. In the 12th century, the Hohenstaufen dynasty provided for a rapid upswing. Frederick Barbarossa and Frederick II both held court in Nuremberg and in

1219 Frederick II granted the city its sovereignty. The city had its own judicial system and began collecting taxes. The Golden Bull in 1356 stated that every newly-elected king was to hold his first court in Nuremberg and like Aachen and Frankfurt, Nuremberg became a Free Imperial City. It also became the royal mint and was under the protection of Egidien Monastery; all these rights were previously reserved to the burgrave who served as the king's administrator. This was reason enough for continual competition between the wealthiest and most influential burghers, the patricians alongside the burgraves who were in charge of the Emperor's lands and fortress in his absence.

A closer study of the fortress complex allows visitors to better understand the rise of the city under the Emperor's protection. In 1040 the Salian fortress stood in the middle of the fortifications where nowadays the Pentagonal Tower stands. This early fortress was given to the burgraves when the Hohenstaufen under Konrad III had a new Imperial fortress erected to the west in 1138. Nowadays, the only remaining evidence of the burgraves' fortress is this same tower and the original Romanesque Walpurgis Chapel.

In 1367 the burghers built a wall around their fortress, which prevented the burgraves direct entry to the city. A mere ten years later, they went a step further and had the so-called Luginsland Tower erected – not as a watchtower for the surrounding countryside as the German name implies: "look into the land," but rather as a city tower that enabled the burghers to have an unobstructed view into the burgraves' courtyard. This tower still stands in the east. Naturally the burghers never bothered to obtain a building permit or consult their neighbors before the tower's construction. In a similar fashion, the burghers sat back

Far left: Sinwell Tower and the entrance to the Deep Well in the foreground.

Left: The Youth Hostel with Luginsland Tower (left) and Pentagonal Tower (right).

Below: The Imperial apartments still display original wainscoting.

and watched as Bavarian troops set fire to the burgraves' fortress during the War of Bavarian Succession in 1420. Seven years later, the burghers acquired the ruinous complex and instead of constructing a new fortress, they had Imperial stables and a granary built. The Pentagonal Tower has been turned into a Youth Center and the royal mews converted into a youth hostel – one of the most charming and popular youth hostels in Germany. Although the fortress complex as well as the city itself was severely damaged in the Second World War, it has been rebuilt to resemble its medieval appearance.

The Builder, Frederick Barbarossa

The Imperial Fortress is located on the western portion of the complex and includes Sinwell Tower (Sin = large, well = round, in Middle High German), the Deep Well, the Double Chapel and palace. Until 1571, every Emperor of the Holy Roman Empire resided within these walls for a period of time. The outer courtyard of the Imperial Fortress including Sinwell Tower and the Deep Well was reserved for the Imperial baggage while the Emperor and his deputies resided in the inner courtyard. Models of varying stages of settlement are on display in the fortress museum. More recent excavations have revealed the foundations of an older round tower.

Konrad III, his successor, Frederick Barbarossa, and his successors were responsible for the splendid expansion of the complex in the 12th century. Medieval wainscoting and ornate wooden ceilings still adorn the Imperial apartments and representational rooms in the double-winged palace with its magnificent Knights' and Emperor's Halls. Paintings, tapestries and furnishings date back to the 16th and 17th centuries.

The Romanesque Double Chapel illustrates the division of social classes in medieval society. Commoners gathered in the dank, dark St. Margaret's Chapel

on the lower level where access was from the Burghof, the outer courtyard. More prominent persons entered the upper level of the chapel with its high altar and Imperial gallery directly from the palace. A square opening connects the two chapels. The adjacent Heidenturm or Heathen's Tower, although badly weathered on the front, derived its name from its heathen sculptural motifs. The Gothic brick addition and the pyramid roof were added later.

The 50-meter Deep Well was dug out of the sandstone cliff and most likely proved useful as early as the 12th century when it supplied the Fortress with drinking water during a siege. Sinwell Tower dates back to the 12th century as well and now serves as a picturesque lookout tower. At one time, the fire department held watch in the tower.

Left: View of the upper Romanesque double chapel in the Fortress.

Above: The lower chapel, which was connected by an opening in the ceiling, was reserved for commoners.

The Enemy
Never Had a Chance

A visit to the fortress gardens is a must. They can be reached either from the entry across from the Pentagonal Tower or from the west, at the end of Am ölberg Lane beneath the Fortress. Despite the busy traffic below, the well-tended gardens offer an oasis of enjoyment and peace and quiet. This later portion of the fortifications is 16th century construction. The Italian, Antonio Fazuni, created this zigzag construction without any dead ground. Bridges and tunnels were arched which prevented the enemy from direct fire.

Visitors to the fortifications will hear the story of Robber Baron Eppelein. The well-heeled nobleman actually did exist and he did carry out his foul works. It is also true that robber barons like him were behind the armed conflicts between princes and cities and threatened the Nuremberg merchants'

convoys and thus the economic prosperity of the flourishing city. The tale that Eppelein managed to escape his own hanging by jumping a 30-meter fortress ditch on horseback is a tall tale. Nonetheless, there are horseshoe imprints on the wall in front of the castle keep and a satirical saying has survived: "The people of Nuremberg don't hang anyone since they have to catch him first." The truth of the matter is that Eppelein was arrested in 1381 and beheaded 50 kilometers south of Nuremberg in the town of Neumarkt.

Above: An evening stroll past St. Sebald's on the left and the Town Hall on the right; the Kaiserburg gazes down from the hill.

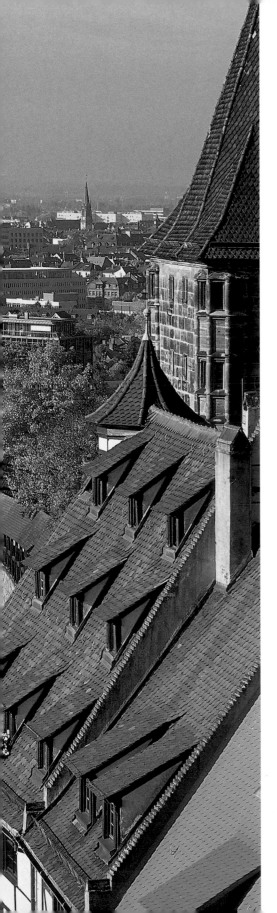

Where Albrecht Dürer Painted and Patricians Danced

The oldest quarter of the city boasts a picturesque square in front of the Dürer House. Museums and the homes of patricians and craftsmen are nearby. St. Sebald's Church is dedicated to the city's patron saint and houses noteworthy art treasures. The Market Square, the Beautiful Fountain and Our Lady's Church give testimony to the glorious days during the reign of Emperor Charles IV.

A Picturesque Square Adorned by a Hare

The square in front of Tiergärtner Gate beneath the Fortress is the most popular and appropriate entry into the city. The Albrecht Dürer House lies to the west; here the master (1471-1528) began living and working as of 1509. At the opposite end of Tiergärtnertor Square, Jürgen Goertz created a caricature of the world famous Dürer hare as a giant endangered plastic monster in 1984. The monster hare proved to pose no real threat to the numerous children who attempted to pet and even climb it. The citizens of the city paid a far more serious tribute to Dürer in 1840 when they commissioned Jacob Daniel Burgschmiet to cast

a monument of Dürer, one of the few in Germany, for Albrecht Dürer Square. Whether it is his field hare or his praying hands, Dürer is everywhere, even on beer coasters in the pub. Whoever has taken the time to peruse Dürer originals – 1,000 sketches, 100 copper etchings, 350 wood carvings, and 70 paintings – will be fascinated by his ingenuity, his precision and the modernity of his work. He dedicated his life to naturalistic drawings and etchings of animate objects; his skillfulness still moves us in the 21st century. Dürer's fondness of painting self-portraits was uncommon at the time. The cosmopolitan disposition of both the Emperor and the commercial city enabled the son of a goldsmith from Hungary to establish himself in Nuremberg. His friendships with Humanists

Previous page: The view from Knights' Hall in the Fortress includes the Pilatus House and Tiergärtner Tower Gate (right) and a portion of the city wall as well as the round New Gate Tower. The Dürer House is in the foreground.

Left: Tiergärtnertor Square in front of the Fortress and the Dürer House to the right front.

Below: Interior views of the Dürer House.

such as Willibald Pirckheimer as well as his travels to Italy and the Netherlands were extremely beneficial. This Renaissance artist wrote knowledgeable textbooks and his individual style characterized an entire epoch known as the Dürer era. The Albrecht Dürer House has been turned into a museum where an audiovisual guide explains the life and work of the master craftsman. In one scene, his wife Agnes appears in original costume and guides visitors through the household to the tune of Dürer rap.

The well-restored four-story building dating back to 1420 provides a good example of a patrician home with its sandstone pedestal base, late medieval half-timbered design and its protruding balcony directly under the roof.

The Pub Scene

From Tiergärtner Gate, Am Ölberg Lane leads up to the Fortress. This narrow street contains some tiny houses that managed to survive the bombing in World War II. In the Middle Ages, these houses were one-story craftsmen's homes to which floors were added over the course of time. Another picture-perfect medieval lane is

Weissgerbergasse or Tanner's Lane a bit farther south. This busy street attracts tourists during the day and in the evenings, the young at heart take a stroll to be a part of the lively pub scene. This is where tawers and tanners treated skins to be turned into leather (look for the tanner's symbol on House Nr. 24). Nuremberg's citizens' action committee, the Friends of the Old Town Association, has been working extremely diligently for years to ensure that many of the buildings here as elsewhere in the Old Town have been faithfully restored to their original condition. Archeological excavations have indicated that the old-

Left: Tiergärtnertor Square is a popular meeting place for young people on warm summer nights.

Above: An old half-timbered structure on the corner of Obere and Untere Krämergasse.

Following pages: An ensemble of narrow craftsmen's homes lines Tanner's Lane. Nowadays these buildings house fancy boutiques and down-home pubs.

das haus der evangelisch-lutherischen kirche

est settlement along the Pegnitz River may have been much earlier than the first written document mentioning Nuremberg by name in 1050.

Tunnels Hewn out of Bare Rock

Beneath the Old Town are two tunnels that lead to Albrecht Dürer Square. These pathways hewn from bare rock are a part of a tunnel system that covers an area of 25,000 square meters and is four-stories deep. Hammers and chisels were the tools that carved the tunnels out of the sandstone and ever since 1380, this space has been used to store beer and to withdraw and transport potable water. A contrived

Left: The City Museum is located in the Fembo House.

Above: Nuremberg's oldest patrician Renaissance building has numerous art treasures on display including the original Apollo Fountain.

Below: Carlo Brentano carried out the Baroque ceiling plasterwork in the Fembo House.

ventilation system along with the stable sandstone walls has ensured this labyrinth under the Fortress a long life. It served as an air raid shelter in World War II.

Another lesser known spot is the Historical Art Bunker in which many art treasures were stored during the war. The "Angelic Salutation" medallion from St. Lorenz's, the Imperial Crown Jewels, a

globe by Martin Behaim, and the Männleinlauf glockenspiel all survived here. This ventilated shelter was built at a time when the Nazis were still predicting eventual victory and no one even considered an Allied bombing attack.

The sole stately patrician edifice unscathed by the war is the Fembo House cater-cornered to the Town Hall. The late Renaissance and Baroque building is named after the Fembo family who owned it in the 19th century. It was most likely designed by Jakob Wolff the Elder for a local merchant at the end of the 16th century. Wolff also built the Fleischbrücke or Butcher's Bridge. Numerous furnishings and décor such as a Baroque plaster ceiling, a spacious ballroom and a wood-paneled ceiling in a reception hall demonstrate the affluence and refined lifestyle of Nuremberg burghers of the period. Nowadays the building serves as the City Museum. A tour of the museum's several floors offers a good audio-visual overview of the history of the city. A Noricama slide and video show compares the past to the present in Nuremberg.

wooden pillars and paneled ceilings. An oriel or second story window perched on a pillar base was added on the west side. A common feature in Nuremberg architecture, the oriel added a dab of décor to an otherwise drab exterior façade and it was often used as a household altar. Nuremberg once boasted 400 such oriels and throughout the city, around 80 have been rebuilt.

One of the loveliest oriels adorns the parsonage of St. Sebald's; the original is on

The outline of the former 14th century Moritz Chapel can be viewed on Sebald Square. It survived until 1944 but over the course of time, the chapel was used for such bizarre purposes as a market hall and storage depot. On the north side of the square stands the reconstructed Schürstab House, originally dating back to the 13th century and named after a patrician family. Portions of the original building were reincorporated into the structure: the vaulting and frescos, the

Above left: A statue of Albrecht Dürer adorns the square bearing the same name. This statue dates back to 1840 and is one of the few in Germany dedicated to this artist.

Left: The rocky pathways at the Dürer Square lead to medieval beer cellars and springs. This was formerly a pickle cellar.

Above and right: The sandstone oriel on the parsonage of St. Sebald's is a copy; the original can be found in the German National Museum. The inner courtyard reveals a wooden gallery and is half-timbered in design.

view in the German National Museum. Portions of the glass are based on designs by Albrecht Dürer. The inner courtyard reveals a wooden gallery and is half-timbered in design.

Pilgrimages to St. Sebald's

A stroll to Egidien Square through the Sebald Quarter goes past the Peller House, an example of 20th century architecture instead of a reconstruction from the past. The current owners, however, are planning to restore the inner courtyard to its former style.

Egidien's Church stands on the east side of the square and is one of the city's rare examples of Baroque architecture. Originally the church started out as a 12th century Romanesque monastery, the oldest in Nuremberg. Destroyed in the 17th century, it was rebuilt to include an ornate vaulted ceiling painting. The

church was refurbished just prior to the Second World War but its destruction was inevitable during the bombing of Nuremberg. Postwar reconstruction eliminated the vaulted ceiling and stuccowork in the sanctuary; the side chapels remain.

St. Sebald's houses the tomb of the city's patron saint and its history is closely linked with Nuremberg's beginnings. On the one hand, the establishment of a royal military stronghold that was first documented in the Sigena Certificate of 1050 encouraged the city's development and its rapid acquirement of the right to hold markets, coin money and collect customs. The second component that

Above: The Bratwursthäusle or Bratwurst Restaurant in front of St. Sebald's emits inviting aromas.
Right: The Gothic nave in St. Sebald's.

36

was to the city's advantage was Pastor Sebald himself, who most likely was a member of a religious movement that was working towards the unleashing of the church from its dependency on nobility. He was said to have lived the life of a hermit in the Imperial Forest and to have died around the middle of the 11th century. It is understandable that very little is actually known about him except for the fact that already during his lifetime, Sebald was venerated as a miraculous healer. Upon his death, the legends about his deeds continued to spread. He was said to have turned icicles into firewood when a miser hid his kindling from him. When a peasant farmer's ox ran off to the woods, Sebald lit the hands of the peasant so that he could search for his ox. During Sebald's funeral procession, it was told that the ox pulling his funeral cart obeyed Sebald's last wish and stopped the procession precisely at the spot the pious

man wished to be buried. This was the future location of St. Sebald's Church.

Pilgrimages to Sebald's tomb contributed considerably to Nuremberg's economic prosperity. Long-term favorable credits to Pope Martin V from the city might have sped up the Pope's decision to canonize Sebald in 1425. During the heydays of the Free Imperial City, St. Sebald was named the patron saint protecting the city from the burgraves and he was also the patron saint of merchants.

The erecting of the Romanesque church began in 1237 and Sebald's relics were placed in a silver shrine. Even after the Reformation when pilgrimages were no longer permitted, his popularity as the city's patron saint remained strong. At the beginning of the 14th century the multitude of pilgrims was so great that the side aisles were widened and several stories were added to the towers which

became High Gothic in style. The east choir was torn down and replaced by a more spacious one with three aisles, an ambulatory and a high altar. Originally, the church had a cemetery until the plague came and the city had it moved to the far side of the city walls. A Baroque interior décor and choir lofts were removed at the beginning of the 20th century and the church was restored to its former appearance. At the end of the Second World War, the towers, roof and choir vaulting were in ruins.

The church houses numerous treasures. The Shrine of the Holy Sacraments behind the high altar dates back to 1370 and it is one of the oldest surviving examples of its kind. The ambry still preserves the original ironwork. The baptismal font is from 1430 and St. Peter's Altar from 1480. The "Prince of the World" on the north side displays a man whose back has been devoured by worms – the symbol of the transitoriness of man. Veit Stoss' three scenes from the Passion from 1499 are in the east choir. St. Sebald's Tomb is from the workshop of the renowned metal founder, Peter Vischer (1460-1529), and

Above: Sebald's Tomb is from the workshop of Peter Vischer who included a depiction of himself (close-up above right) in this masterpiece.

Left: The marvelous organ in St. Sebald's is the focus of attention every spring during International Organ Week.

Sebald's reliquary is enclosed in a late Gothic three-vault baldachin. The filigree adornment was probably carried out by Peter Vischer the Younger, who created prophets, saints and apostles as well as deities, putti angels, mermaids, dolphins and snails in the Renaissance style. The self-confident artist also immortalized himself in one of the figures. Brass relief retells the legend of Sebald: healing the blind, the icicle and wine miracles and the conversion of the heretic. These are powerful portrayals that have lost none of their significance in today's world.

Proud Patricians

Although the inhabitants of Nuremberg were avid followers of the Reformation early on, they refrained from destroying the veneration of the saints in St. Sebald's, St. Lorenz's and elsewhere.

Above: The Great Hall in the Town Hall boasts a lovely wooden ceiling while its walls remain white due to the fact that the inhabitants could never agree on how it was to be painted.
Right: The Town Hall's imposing façade across from the second story oriel of St. Sebald's Church.

These sacred art treasures had been gifts from the city's patrician class and the city fathers insisted on maintaining "their" monuments. Who exactly were these patricians, the movers and shakers who determined the fate of their city from the beginning of its independence in the 14th century until it became a

part of Bavaria in 1806? Patricians were members of nobility that emerged from the class of administrative officials that originally served the Emperor. Patrician families had their own coats-of arms and knightly titles; they acquired land outside the city and were merchants and councilmen who ran an oligarchic form of government that, despite an uproar from the guilds in 1348, excluded craftsmen from becoming a part of the municipal administration.

This patrician display of self-confidence is easy to decipher on the west façade of the Town Hall across from St. Sebald's.

Jakob Wolff the Younger designed the public building in 1616. A pelican above the entrance symbolizes the selfless devotion of the councilmen to their city. The letters PLEG are a German abbreviation for "We govern by means of intelligence, law and mercy." Figures representing the world of Antiquity above the northern and southern entrances remind pass-ers-by that Nuremberg was one of the Free Imperial Cities in the Holy Roman Empire of the German Nation. At first glance, the building, inspired by the Italian Renaissance, is less impressive due to its proximity to St. Sebald's. The Thirty Years' War prevented all four wings of the structure from being completed. The Gothic Great Hall is a part of the older

portion of the complex; however, the sumptuous wall paintings stipulated by Dürer and Willibald Pirckheimer have long since disappeared.

In the 1980s the inhabitants of Nuremberg decided to have the barren walls of the Great Hall painted by a former local artist whose history studies and artistic abilities could have reproduced a medieval design. Michael Mathias Prechtl (1926-2003), well-known worldwide for

Below: A sea of rooftops and more towers: Tucher Castle (right front), Egidien Church (middle) and St. Sebald's (back right). To the left in the background: Plärrer high rise, St. Elizabeth's, White Tower and St. Jakob's.

his original and intelligent history book illustrations, had already sketched scenes for the façade depicting the glorious as well as the tragic days in the history of the city. The plan was never realized and it seems that the local prophet who was not recognized in his own hometown distanced himself entirely from the city.

Copies of the Imperial Crown Jewels are exhibited in the Hall of Fame in the Town Hall. These were the jewels emperors displayed when they were visiting Nuremberg. The approach of French troops in 1796 made it necessary to take the original Imperial crown, scepter and orb via Regensburg to Vienna to a secure place. Over two hundred years later, they remain safe and sound in the Weltliche Schatzkammer in Vienna.

The fact that patricians served as judges in the Town Hall made it essential to turn the cellar into a huge dungeon. Twelve surviving prison cells can be toured.

Toys from Nuremberg

First and foremost, Nuremberg is world famous for its tiny sausages or bratwurst and Lebkuchen or gingerbread. However, its Toy Fair with exhibitors from 70 countries and approximately a million items on display makes this the largest toy fair worldwide. The Middle Ages was a creative era for Nuremberg merchants and craftsmen who were known for their

Left: Egidien Church was originally Romanesque until it was rebuilt in the Baroque style in the 17th century.

Above: The Toy Museum is a vibrant reminder of the skilled craftsmen and commercial tradition associated with Nuremberg. The statue in the foreground is by Michael Prechtl.

inventions of useful gadgets and young and old alike had a penchant for games. Industrialization combined the city's expertise and commercial tradition to manufacture "Nuremberg trinkets" such as mechanical toys, tops, trumpets, dollhouse porcelain, steam engines, metal erector sets and trains. The toy industry employed 8,000 people in 1910. The Jewish Bing brothers, who were expelled during the Third Reich, owned the world's largest toy company. Nuremberg was equally renowned for printing children's books and manufacturing tin figures. Nowadays a few model train companies such as Fleischmann, LGB and Trix are all that remain of the boom days of the past. Playmobil, Big and Carrera are the major toy manufacturers in the larger Nuremberg area.

After the First World War, at a time when toys were not yet considered culturally and historically significant, Lydia and Paul Beyer began collecting. The Toy Museum first opened its doors in the

1970s in the Karlstrasse and offers a comprehensive overview of the 1,000-year history and importance of toys. Nuremberg's role in toy manufacturing is extremely well-documented.

The Glockenspiel at the Market Square

Once the largest paved square north of the Alps, the Market Square in Nuremberg is still the center of the tourist industry especially during the Advent season when the Christkindl Market attracts thousands of visitors. Fresh produce from the surrounding region is sold throughout the year, but the main attraction is the Männleinlauf or strutting men at the glockenspiel at Our Lady's Church. At 12

Left side: View of the Market Square with the Fleischbrücke or Butcher's Bridge in the foreground. Erected on wooden pylons, the bridge somewhat resembles the Rialto in Venice although it is much sturdier. The stone ox on the bridge bears the inscription: "was never a calf." Such sayings are typical of dry Franconian humor and Franconian even-temperedness.

Right: Tourists in front of the Beautiful Fountain at the Market Square watch the glockenspiel depicting Charles IV being greeted by his seven electors at Our Lady's Church.

Below: Just one of the many details of the Beautiful Fountain: turning the golden ring promises not only good luck but also a horde of children.

noon, a door opens and two trumpeters announce the appearance of Emperor Charles IV. Seven marching men, the electors dressed in red, pay tribute to the presence of the Emperor. The glocken-spiel is reminiscent of the Golden Bull of 1356 in which Emperor Charles IV decreed that the king was to be elected by these very same electors and that every newly-elected emperor had to hold the first day of his Imperial Diet in Nuremberg. Charles IV visited the city a total of 45 times and often stayed months at a time.

Both the Market Square and Our Lady's Church are the infamous doings of Charles IV. Originally the square was the hub of the Jewish quarter, a marshy piece of land near the Pegnitz that the Jewish community had drained and made inhabitable. After the first pogrom in 1298 during which 628 Jews were murdered, the Sebald and Lorenz quarters were advancing toward each other across the Pegnitz. The square was more or less in the way. Emperor Charles, the patron of the tax-paying Jews, indirectly gave his permission for another pogrom in order to create a central Market Square for the selling of produce. During the pogrom of 1349, around one-third of the Jewish population (562 Jews) died. Out Lady's Church was erected as a court chapel for the emperor on the site of the synagogue and several patrician families bought prime property near the Market Square. A final expulsion took place in 1498/99. For the next 350 years, Jews were not permitted to live or even spend the night in Nuremberg.

The court architect from Prague, Peter Parler, was most likely responsible for the design of the Gothic Our Lady's Church or Frauenkirche. Mary, Mother of God, can be seen in countless paintings and

Left: The Beautiful Fountain at the Market Square resembles a Gothic spire with its forty figures and pinnacle. Our Lady's Church forms the backdrop.

sculptures. Michael's Choir, which is actually a tiny chapel above the narthex was designed by Adam Kraft. Both Kraft and Michael Wohlgemut were responsible for several of the epitaphs. Three stained glass windows portraying St. Paul, St. Christopher and Mary are a part of the former Emperor's Window which Charles IV donated.

The Frauenkirche or Our Lady's Church dates back to 1355 and is considered to be the third most important church in the city. It is also the oldest example of a hall church in Franconia. Upon secularization in 1803, the church lost most of its original furnishings and relics. Catholics replaced these losses with religious treasures from the surrounding

cian family, displays the Annunciation, Crucifixion, and the Risen Christ and is considered a masterpiece of 15th century panel painting in Nuremberg.

monasteries. After the church was destroyed during World War II, it was rebuilt as an almost perfectly square hall church reminiscent of the original 14th century house of God. The High Altar was salvaged from St. Augustine's, which was torn down in 1816. This so-called Tucher altar, named after a wealthy patri-

Left and center close-up: Every day at noon, tourists and locals alike gather at Our Lady's Church to watch the Männleinlauf glockenspiel during which seven strutting men pay tribute to Emperor Charles IV. This over-sized glockenspiel is a major attraction on the Market Square where fresh local produce is sold year round.

Above: The Frauenkirche or Our Lady's Church is the oldest example of a hall church in Franconia. Almost perfectly square in shape, the Catholic sanctuary is adorned with numerous sculptures and paintings of Our Lady, the Virgin Mary.

A World-Famous Fountain

Another work of the Gothic is the Schöner Brunnen or Beautiful Fountain at the opposite end of the square. It is a 19-meter high gilded and painted pyramid that was originally out of sandstone and later, shell limestone; the original is in the German National Museum. The fountain base is square and the pyramid rises like a spire culminating in a finial. The 40 figures adorning the fountain represent the world of the Holy Roman Empire of the German Nation. Starting at the lower level, there is philosophy and the arts; above them, the evangelists and church fathers followed by the seven electors and nine heroes. Moses and seven prophets are at the upper level. The charming latticework has a ring that turns. Newly-

weds emerging from the church as well as knowledgeable visitors turn the ring as it is said to promise to bring good luck and a multitude of children.

Lebkuchen and Mulled Wine

The Beautiful Fountain, Our Lady's Church and the Market Square are products of the late Middle Ages during the successful reign of Charles IV. Up until their destruction in the Second World War, patrician homes adorned the square where every Easter the Imperial Crown Jewels were ceremoniously presented.

Nowadays, the Market Square boasts its greatest grandeur during the Christmas season when the Christkindl Market with its countless red-and-white striped booths attracts a million tourists from all corners of the globe. Whether it be the enticing smell of bratwurst or the spicy, gingerbread-like Lebkuchen that draws the crowds, one thing is certain: since 1628 the market has been selling little wooden Christmas boxes. Originally, 140

Above left: An evening view of the delightful Christmas booths on the Market Square with the Beautiful Fountain in the foreground and Our Lady's Church to the rear.

Left: These cheerful "prune figures" are made of nuts and various dried fruit.

Above: The Christkind angel and her two helpers officially open the Christkindl Christmas Market.

tradesmen came to peddle their wares; the number remains fairly constant even today. Since 1948 an angel standing on the balcony of Our Lady's Church has officially opened the Christkindl Market with a poem. Now as before, unique Christmas ornaments, straw stars and angels made of glossy paper or wax, nuts and dried fruit including the "little prune man" make up the typical Nuremberg fare. Back in 1610 the councilmen banned the "inappropriate articles" of a wood turner. This ban still manages to have its repercussions: plastic Christmas trees, cheesy knickknacks, flashy fashion items and carousels are not a part of this market.

The Home of a Patrician Family

A walk through the old part of Sebald quarter is definitely worthwhile. Patrician homes like Tucher Castle display period furniture and tapestries as well as other important works of art. Hirsvogel Hall from 1534 is located in the gardens and has recently been restored. It is one of the

loveliest Renaissance halls in Germany. The Tucher family remodeled the castle and its park-like grounds in the Renaissance style in 1544 and it became their summer residence. Nevertheless, several other architectural styles are evident: Nuremberg late Gothic, Italian Renaissance, and French palatial design. The castle museum acquaints visitors with the opulent life of an influential patrician family in the 16th century. Hirsvogel Hall contains a richly-decorated wooden wall covering by Peter Flötner as well a magnificent ceiling painting by Georg Pencz, a student of Dürer's. The Renaissance gardens surrounding the castle and hall isolate this oasis from the rest of the Old Town.

The Tucher Castle brings to life the importance of such a patrician family and makes clear the significant role the councilmen played in the city's economic development. Patrician families from outside Nuremberg were welcomed but only one family of craftsmen was permitted to settle in the city. By 1521 newcomers of any stripe were no longer admitted to the city and a so-called dance statute strictly regulated precisely who was allowed to attend balls in the Town Hall and who could rule the roost. Such narrow-minded politics eventually contributed to the city's economic downfall which lasted until the 19th century.

Left: The lifestyle enjoyed by the patricians can be experienced in Tucher Castle.

Below: Hirsvogel Hall from 1534 was rebuilt in the Renaissance style in the castle garden.

Where Hans Sachs Sang and Kasper Hauser Made an Appearance

The Pegnitz River divides the city into two distinct quarters. Picturesque bridges, green islets and weirs lend the city a romantic ambience similar to what Dürer once painted. The Holy Ghost Charitable Institution was built by the city's wealthiest inhabitant. The mysterious foundling, Kasper Hauser, first appeared to the world in Nuremberg.

The Holy Ghost Charitable Institution

The Pegnitz River divides Nuremberg's two oldest quarters: Sebald and Lorenz. The two quarters were first linked in 1320 by the Heubrücke or Hay Bridge in the east and by Hangman's Footbridge in the west. Floods in the Old Town like the one in 1909 no longer pose a threat.

Two pedestrian bridges south of the Market Square lead from the Sebald quarter into the Lorenz quarter. From the Museum Bridge looking east beyond the shop windows and booths, the Holy Ghost Charitable Institution appears through the trees with the Pegnitz flowing beneath it. The marshy grounds were drained and in 1331, the charitable institution became a home for the old and the frail; it still performs these functions. The merchant and councilman, Konrad Gross (circa 1280-1356) founded the charitable institution for 200 patients. For years it was the largest institution of this type donated by an individual burgher. By the 18th century it

had acquired numerous pieces of property within the city walls as well as 700 farmsteads in 150 towns and villages in the surrounding area. In times of emergency, the city took out loans from this charitable institution. It remains the richest charitable institution in Nuremberg.

Konrad Gross, (the man gave himself this name: gross = great), lies buried beneath an unusual table tombstone next to statues by Adam Kraft in the Kreuzigungshof Courtyard. His benevolence and social-political perspective were only one aspect of this successful merchant's worldly outlook. The most affluent man in Nuremberg was the financier of Emperor Ludwig the Bavarian of the Wittelsbach dynasty. In the 16th century, the Holy Ghost Charitable Institution was one of the places that Hans Sachs (1494-1576), the renowned minnesinger and poet, performed. A monument to this famous inhabitant of Nuremberg can be found on the square bearing his name, which just happens to be in front of the charitable institution. The poet wrote 10,000

songs, poems and plays. During the summer months, theater groups dig out and perform some of his sketches on everyday life in medieval times. Sachs, a musically-talented shoemaker, who was basically a folksy propagandist of the Reformation, was immortalized by Richard Wagner in the 19th century in his opera, "Die Meistersänger von Nürnberg."

Once a Synagogue

The silhouette of a synagogue is engraved in a monument to the south of Hans-Sachs Square in front of the bridge. It was dedicated in 1874 when Jews were once again permitted to settle in Nuremberg. The Nazi party boss, Julius Streicher, had the monument torn down in August 1938, months before the pogroms of Kristallnacht on November 9th of that same year.

Just before the Hay Bridge to the south, there is the Männerschuldturm, a tower that has been turned into a Franconian garden restaurant. The name, which roughly translates as Guilty Men Tower, is a reminder

that the city towers along the walls once doubled as prisons. Debtors and the mentally unstable were imprisoned there. The artificial island adjacent divides the river into two arms and in July, it is the meeting place for poet gatherings and in the fall, it serves as the venue for the Old Town Festival. The island, a result of soil deposits, has a long tradition of fairs and German marksmen's celebrations where only a few of the actual revelers are marksmen. A new footbridge leads to a new entertainment complex that attracts young people from far and wide on the weekends: the multiplex cinema Cinecitta with 18 theaters and IMAX and MAD cinemas. Anchored deep in the ground on the banks of the

Previous pages: The Holy Ghost Charitable Institution seen from Museum Bridge.

Left: Hans Sachs, the shoemaker-poet, is seated in the square bearing his name in front of the Holy Ghost Charitable Institution.

Below: A view of the southern side of the Holy Ghost Charitable Institution on the Pegnitz; the Guilty Men Tower and Hay Bridge are to the right.

Pegnitz, the airy glass and aluminum structure blends in with its surroundings along the river. The views of the Fortress and the medieval towers and walls from the terraces of the complex are breathtaking.

The Fleischbrücke or Butcher's Bridge leading from the Market Square to the Lorenz quarter was the most heavily traveled route in medieval times. Flooding destroyed the abutments numerous times. It wasn't until 1598 that the bridge was constructed as a single arch, similar to the Rialto Bridge in Venice. The bridge's name is a reminder that butchers slaughtered their animals at their stalls located on the Market Square into the 20th century. They offered their wares at the butchery on the Pegnitz. The arched gate next to the butchery leads to a path along the north bank. The horned, stone ox above the arch is not there by acci-

dent. The inhabitants of Nuremberg are of the opinion that this ox symbolizes their Franconian stoic composure. The ox is also reported to have heard many a strange tale in his time but he never utters a sound. As the saying in Latin on the base reveals, this ox was never a calf.

The Weinstadel building, which lies a bit further northwest, served students meals for years until it was renovated into small apartments not too long ago. The 15th century sandstone construction with its two half-timbered stories, wooden galleries and water spouts formerly served lepers who were normally banned from within the medieval walls. However, during the Holy Week each year, lepers received medical assistance and were served hearty meals due to special infirmity alms.

The Foundling, Kasper Hauser

Cross Hangman's Footbridge to the Lorenz quarter to Unschlitt Square with the Bagpipe Player Fountain. The dominating building here is the Unschlitthaus, one of the city's former granaries; nowadays it houses a pawnshop. A pleasant ensemble of 16th and 17th century craftsmen's homes again enhances the square; the Friends of the Old Town Association was able to save these buildings from being torn down in order to widen the street. House Nr. 8 with a Madonna on the corner is where the foundling Kasper Hauser was discovered over Pentecost in 1828. The backward 16-year old spoke a strange tongue and rumors concerning his whereabouts immediately spread like wildfire. He was thrown into the Luginsland prison tower at the Fortress and then over time, several guardians attempted to educate him. Strange circumstances were behind his murder in the court gardens in Ansbach in 1833. After over a hundred years of speculation and research including DNS analysis, the origins of the young man continue to remain a mystery. According to genetic analysts, he might have been the illegitimate son of one of the princes of Baden. Historians believe he could have been the illegitimate son of a Tyrolean member of the occupation forces. The inhabitants of Nuremberg have named a square after him in a new apartment development. A new high rise with a Franconian gable roof is to imply the symbiosis between the medieval and the modern.

Above: The Pegnitz River is as picturesque as when Dürer painted it: the half-timbered Weinstadel and the Water Tower to the left of Hangman's Footbridge.

A glimpse of the Pegnitz and the Ketten-steg or Chain Footbridge to the west offers a satisfying view. Erected in 1824 and suspended on chains, it was Germany's first suspension bridge across a river. Early on, the bridge was used by children wanting to add a little adventure to their lives, much to the displeasure of their parents. In 1931, the fun was halted by additional wooden pillars and iron supports. At present, a team of architects is trying to restore the bridge to its original swaying condition. It was truly an elegant landmark in its day.

Strolls along the Pegnitz River are not only pleasurable within the Old Town. West of the Chain Footbridge is the so-called Hallenwiese, a park-like area that passes a restored mill and waterworks on its way to the Johannis quarter and even further, to the city of Fürth. Heading east, a bike route along the river take the visitor to many scenic and cultural attractions such as Lake Wöhrder, the village of Mögeldorf and its historical center, the Oberbürg castle ruin and the village of Hammer, a well-preserved hamlet whose origins date back to the early industrial period.

Right and below: Chain Bridge was the first suspension bridge in Germany (1824). Both seniors and students reside within the city walls at Haller Gate.

Museums, Monasteries and Three Renowned Artisans

The German National Museum is the home of the largest collection of German art and culture. The New Museum displays modern art and design. St. Lorenz's Parish Church houses the treasures of three great artisans: Adam Kraft, Peter Vischer, and Veit Stoss.

Germany's Largest National Museum

The German National Museum's collections could actually fill several museums and it remains the ideal place to study Nuremberg's history and culture. In 1494, at a time when Columbus was undertaking his voyages to the Americas, Martin Behaim, a navigator and geographer, created the oldest surviving globe of the Earth. For many years it stood proudly in the Town Hall as a symbol of new discoveries and endeavors. The globe was constructed out of a ball of loam and covered with thin strips of linen and parchment paper. Marco Polo's travels were recorded as well as valuable information from a fellow Humanist from Nuremberg, Hart-

mann Schedel. Schedel's Chronicle of the World (as of 1487) appeared in Latin and German and was a masterpiece of early book printing with its 1800 woodcuts. Famous sketchers such as Michael Wohlgemut and Wilhelm Pleydenwurff assisted. The Chronicle was to present known facts about the world beginning with the Bible and concluding with contemporary Humanist theories of the time. The woodcut of Nuremberg depicted in the book became the model for several other medieval cities for many years. Regiomontanus, the most renowned mathematician and astronomer of the late Middle Ages, moved to Nuremberg in 1471 because the best meters and gauges were produced there. The museum has a collection of his sun-dials and clockworks and other inventive instruments used to measure time as well as some of his astro-

logical instruments. One of the oldest tower clocks and a pocket watch belonging to Peter Henlein whose improved version became a worldwide success are also worth noting.

Although only a few of Albrecht Dürer's paintings hang in this museum, the most extensive collection of works by Veit Stoss is within these walls as well as other old masters such as Albrecht Altdorfer, Lukas Cranach, Peter Vischer, Tilman Riemenschneider and Rembrandt.

In an area covering 50,000 m², the museum exhibits artifacts dating from 30,000 BCE to the present day: everything from coins, musical instruments, sculpture and folklore to weapons, toys and works of art from varying periods. Early in his youth, Baron Hans von Aufsess (1801–1872) began collecting old

books and documents from paper mills, altar panels and silver from secularized monasteries and nunneries as well as weapons and furniture from dilapidated fortress ruins. King Ludwig I of Bavaria encouraged the baron to put his treasures on public display and in 1857, the king purchased the monastery grounds in the Old Town for him. Even though national unity had not been attained, this museum was to present the historical and ideal unity of Germany. At the

Previous pages: White columns flank the front of the German National Museum and form the Street of Human Rights.

Above: The former Carthusian Monastery has been incorporated into the German National Museum, the largest museum for German culture and art.

two styles can coexist. A further addition to this ensemble, the Street of Human Rights by the Israeli artist, Dani Karavan, has found a home here as well. The United Nations' Articles of Human Rights have been carved into thirty white columns in German and numerous other languages. This passageway was created in 1995, the first time the International Human Rights Award was bestowed on Nuremberg.

Instead of the obligatory busts so commonly found in 19th century museums, the narrow passageway to Luitpold Street displays the names of five of Nuremberg's most famous citizens: Dürer, Veit Stoß, Hans Sachs and two philosophers, Hegel

time, the adjective "German" referred solely to the historical and geographic borders of German-speaking countries.

The Street of Human Rights

The German National Museum offers a comprehensive, historical overview of Nuremberg and the surrounding environs. Its postmodern expansion constructed of glass, steel and concrete nicely complements the medieval architecture surrounding it, proving that the

Above: Exhibits on display in the German National Museum in former cloisters of a monastery.

Right: The inner courtyard of the museum is a popular venue for artists and performers alike during the cultural night known as Blue Night.

Following pages: The Street of Human Rights accentuates the lower level of the German National Museum.

and Feuerbach. Georg Wilhelm Friedrich Hegel was the director of Egidien High School as of 1808. His student, Ludwig Feuerbach, is buried in St. Johannis Cemetery outside the city walls.

The Craftsmen's Quarter

After perusing the medieval world of science and skilled craftsmanship in the German National Museum, a visit to the Craftsmen's Quarter behind Klarissen Square is in order. Nestled along narrow streets and surrounded by medieval towers, numerous workshops, craft booths and restaurants present their wares and fare in an atmospheric Old World setting.

Artisans such as tinsmiths and pewterers, metalwork toymakers, potters, gold and silversmiths, glass engravers and painters work alongside gingerbread bakers and doll makers. The quarter is reminiscent of bygone days when Nuremberg's craftsmanship was at its peak: everything from knifes and razors, to funnels and weapons, to locks and wire, clocks and jewelry, to thimbles and compasses. Apprentices and craftsmen were attracted to Nuremberg from early on due to the city's reputation for high quality. There was even a municipal office that not only furnished strict directives but also kept track of the number of artisans and the quality of their wares.

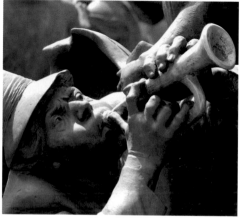

long past, the visitor can once again enter the city via the White Tower even though the passageway is now subterranean. The large fountain is a good place to image what the beginnings of the Lorenz quarter were like: two arms of a fishing stream ran straight through Karolinenstrasse and Breite Gasse. The stream originated to the south and emptied into the Pegnitz at the Karlsbrücke or Charles Bridge. The stream was a source of water for the numerous mills in the city as well as a water supply for artisans. Imperial officials and administrators resided near the fortress in the Sebald quarter while craftsmen and day laborers, merchants and servants made their home in the Lorenz quarter south

The Marriage Fountain and the White Tower

Every inhabitant from Nuremberg and the surrounding areas knows that the White Tower designates the metro station and the beginning of the pedestrian zone. This sandstone tower, a remnant of the fortifications from the 13th century, was once painted white. The barbican portion of the fortifications wasn't reconstructed until 1977 when the metro system was in the planning. As in times

Right and close-up: The Marriage Fountain in front of White Tower is named after the poem "The Bittersweet Conjugal Life" written by Hans Sachs, and dedicated to his wife. The fountain portrays sculptor Jürgen Weber's interpretation of this medieval poem.

of the Pegnitz. Both quarters were established by the king.

Until the 19th century, groundwater drawn from wells was the source of drinking water in the city. Hanselbrunnen at the Holy Ghost Charitable Institution and Hiserleinbrunnen on Unschlitt Square are two such fountains that have survived. The over-sized Ehebrunnen or Marriage Fountain in front of the White Tower was erected in the 1980s to conceal a metro shaft. Based on a poem by Hans Sachs, the marriage carousel by Jürgen Weber was, in the beginning, controversial due to the droll statues adorning it. In the meantime, tastes have changed and the fountain doubles as a kiddy pool on hot summer days. Parents watching over their offspring may take the opportunity to reflect on their own marriages.

A few streets further along is yet another example of the confluence of old and new. The New Museum on Klarissen Square right behind the city walls is the design of the Berlin architect, Volker Staab. His flowing 100-meter large wall of glass reflects the silhouette of the Old Town while simultaneously serving as a giant display window for the art and design in the museum. Entry is from the city walls or down many narrow, winding streets through the Old Town itself. Finally, the view opens up onto

the square where the clarity and transparency of the structure becomes evident and surprisingly appropriate. The New Museum displays internationally known contemporary artists as well as a 20th century design collection.

Two Churches Adorn Jakob Square

Two churches dominate Jakobsplatz: the Protestant St. Jakob's (St. James' in English) and the Catholic St. Elizabeth's.

Both bear witness to the founding of the Lorenz quarter and to the close link between secular and religious politics. Emperor Otto IV bequeathed his royal estate to the German Order who had both St. Jakob's and St. Elizabeth Charitable Institution erected. After the Reformation, the knightly order was permitted to maintain a Catholic enclave in the city even though masses were held behind locked doors and Catholics had no citizens' rights. St. Elizabeth's, the sole remaining church in Nuremberg built in the Classical style, was not consecrated until 1905. Nuremberg's police headquarters are now located on the grounds of the former charitable institution. St. Jakob's, built in 1290, became Protes-

Left: White Tower with its barbicans is in the center.

Above: St. Elizabeth's Catholic Church (left) faces St. Jakob's Protestant Church (right).

Close-up: The dome of St. Elizabeth's from the interior.

tant in 1532 and in 1824 took on its neo-Gothic appearance.

The Carthusian Monastery, erected in the 14th century by a patrician family after a plague, has survived fairly well although, as of 1525, it no longer served as a monastery due to the fact that the majority of its monks became Protestant. The original interior décor has not been preserved but the building itself managed to withstand time and it has become fully integrated into the German Nation Museum.

A Superb Rose Window

The best view of St. Lorenz's Church is from the Karolinenstrasse and and Nassauer House. The rose window on the west facade is around ten meters in diameter. Its eight axes of stone tracery are neither horizontal nor vertical and the window itself seems to roll like a wheel. It was modeled after similar rose windows in northern France and there is nothing like it in all of Franconia. The west portal below displays the Mother of God and the Childhood of Jesus as well as the Last Judgment in the arches above. Adam and Eve are depicted on the sides as well as St. Laurentius, the patron saint of the church.

The church's interior is a treasure trove of medieval art. A special guidebook is essential to fully appreciate these works. Dürer and three further, major Renaissance artists are well-represented within these walls: Adam Kraft, Peter Vischer and Veit Stoss.

The church caretaker, Hans Imhoff, commissioned Adam Kraft (circa 1460-1508)

to design the late Gothic Tabernacle to house the Eucharist. On a column north of the high altar, the slender, spiring structure carved out of local light gray sandstone rises 18.7 meters into the vault. Exquisite thorn-like carvings enhance this tracery in stone and fine gold ironwork adorns the pyx. St. Lorenz

and St. Sebald are featured higher up the pyramid as well as scenes from Christ's Passion culminating in the Crucifixion and Resurrection. An age of new self-confidence is manifested in the crouching figures at the base: Kraft, the stone-carver, and two of his assistants look

Above left: The Craftsmen's Quarter in Königsstrasse features glass-cutters and goldsmiths, puppet-makers and Lebkuchen bakers.

Left: The glass façade of the New Museum at Klarissen Square; the interior focuses on art and design.

Above: The glass façade of the New University outside the city walls at Max Gate.

tral Europe with epitaphs, religious art, medallions and plaques. These beauti-fully-crafted works of art document the changes in taste from the late Gothic to the Renaissance. Vischer's most renowned work was the Sebald Tomb in St. Sebald's. His sons worked with him on the shrine between 1508 and 1519.

Hanging in the middle of the choir, the Angelic Salutation by Veit Stoss (circa 1448-1533) remains his most acclaimed work. The linden wood medallion poig-nantly depicts the Annunciation. The larger-than-life figures of Archangel Gabriel and the Virgin Mary come to life as Mary, upon hearing the news, lifts

Above: The Fountain of Virtues on Lorenz Square represents the seven virtues including love, hope and patience, crowned by justice.

Below: The Nassauer House in front of St. Lorenz's is the sole remaining well-preserved tower house in the city.

Right: The rose window of St. Lorenz's seen from the Nassauer House and Karolinerstrasse.

openly proud of their accomplishments. Youth and experience worked side by side to create a masterpiece.

Adam Kraft most likely completed his apprenticeship in Nuremberg during the building of the choir of St. Lorenz's. Much of his work can still be viewed throughout the city: the Strangulation of Beatrice in St. Lorenz's, the Schreyer-Landau epitaph in the east choir of St. Sebald's, the Peringsdörfer epitaph in Our Lady's Church and the Gothic portal bearing the city's coat-of-arms on the east side of the Mauthalle or Customs House. Kraft's Stations of the Cross, which origi-nally led from Tiergärtner Gate to the Johannis Cemetery are now housed in the German National Museum and the Holy Ghost Charitable Institution.

Peter Vischer the Elder (circa 1460-1529) was a friend of Kraft's. His master crafts-man's piece was the bronze chandelier in the nave of St. Lorenz's. The Vischer family ran a foundry that supplied Cen-

78

her hand in astonishment and drops the book she is reading. The intricacy and plasticity of the drapery and the curly locks and the noble attention to detail are incredible. Fifty-five roses adorn the wreath and seven small medallions retell of the event. God the Father holding the orb in one hand crowns the portrayal while the Serpent whispers to the forbidden fruit below. Full appreciation of this work of art includes the skillfully carved sun and moon symbolizing the worldwide significance of Gabriel's message that can be seen on the back side.

Veit Stoss was a sculptor, copper engraver and woodcarver. He came from the town of Horb on the Neckar River and before settling in Nuremberg, he learned his trade in several European cities. Well-established in Nuremberg, in 1477 he moved to Crakow, Poland, for nineteen years to carve the splendid Virgin Mary Altar in St. Mary's. Although he had a flourishing workshop in Nuremberg as of 1496, the city council convicted him of fraud and had him publicly branded on both cheeks. Public stigmatization proved enormous and Emperor Maximilian I pardoned him. In gratification, Stoss, at the age of seventy, created the Angelic Salutation, the Chandelier of the Madonna and a Crucifix for St. Lorenz's.

The sole remaining example of a well-preserved medieval tower house is the Nassauer House on the west side of Lorenz Square. Both the ground and first floors date back to the early 13th century. In the 15th century, the upper floors with their oriel and battlements embellished by four octagonal corner towers and steep roof were added. Since King Sigismund had pledged one of his crowns for a period of time to the wealthy owner, the owner had the stone balustrade decorated with the coats-of arms of the Emperor, the Pope, the seven electors and the Free Imperial City. The tower's martial appearance was, from the very beginning, more symbolic than threatening. The Nassauer Keller, a charming subterranean restaurant with a medieval vault, is open to the public.

Left: The Angelic Salutation, the carved portrayal of the Annunciation by Veit Stoss, hangs in the middle of the choir of St. Lorenz's.

Above: The Angelic Salutation with the Virgin and Gabriel.

Close-up left: The stone-carver, Adam Kraft, bears the weight of the 19-meter tall Tabernacle.

The Destination of Germany's First Railroad

Johannis Cemetery outside the Old Town is one of Europe's most enchanting. The Opera House and the German Rail Museum as well as the Museum for Industrial Culture are representative of the city's development into modernity. The Nazi Party Rally Grounds are a testimony to Hitler's delusions of grandeur.

From Dürer's Grave to Modernity

Johannis Cemetery located in Johannis quarter west of the Old Town contains several of Europe's most beautiful and culturally-historical graves. The uniformity of the sandstone tombs decorated with large urns of flowers enhances the individual bronze epitaphs. The engravings, craftsmen's chisel marks, coats-of-arms and base relief reveal the professions, fates and social class of individual families such as in the case of the goldsmith, Hans Bauch (German for belly), who transports his paunch in a wheelbarrow. Hard rolls, pretzels and bread tell the tragic story of a baker's family with 20 children, only 5 of whom survived their parents (crosses on their heads). One patrician has a nail embedded in his skull; his wife is said to have driven it in while he slept.

The Humanist Willibald Pirckheimer once said, "Virtue doesn't die." Allegorical female figures accompany the goldsmith, Wenzel

Jamnitzer, to his grave and Albrecht Dürer expressed the following wish: "Earth was minutely detailed; now Heaven has you." Veit Stoss was only permitted a brass plaque with his name on it and the family of industrial capitalists, the Cramer-Klett family, is represented by a monument constructed solely of iron. The director of the first German railroad, Johannes Scharrer, lies buried not far from his English locomotive driver, William Wilson.

Previous pages: Patricians used Baroque Gardens like this one in Johannisstrasse to grow exotic fruits.

Above left: A statue from the Baroque Garden located at Johannisstrasse 13.

Above right: Albrecht Dürer's gravestone.

Left: Johannis Cemetery is famous for its pleasant arrangement of flat gravestones that offer serene tranquility year round.

The Opera House

The Opera House in Nuremberg erected in 1905 is at the edge of the Old Town – an extension of the Street of Human Rights. The opera was built next to the train station which had already been completed in 1847. The arrival of the train helped the adjacent Lorenz quarter develop into a modern complex containing hotels, museums, shops and tourism. The Sebald quarter further north maintained its historical quaintness with the fortress, patrician homes and Town Hall.

The Opera House offers more than just operas; it is the venue of the annual Nuremberg Opera Ball, the Blue Night event (culture throughout the city) and the Night of Ballroom Dancing. Businesses rent it out for their receptions and festivities and car dealerships and insurance companies are eager sponsors. The Opera House has once again become a center of cultural events and refined entertainment.

Nuremberg, the home of the Meistersingers, wanted to erect a suitable cultural center that documented the industrial upswing that the city was enjoying. A steel skeleton incorporating the latest construction technology was concealed by a sandstone façade and historicized ornamentation. Nordic gods and the Three Fates flank the façade and entrance. The nymph Noris, the fictive goddess of Nuremberg, crowns the gable and is surrounded by the councilmen and Meistersingers.

The interior is pure Jugendstil or art nouveau. Hitler had the grotto fountain and other gems on the first floor removed in 1935; they were too decadent for his taste. He preferred his own style at the opening of the annual Nazi Party Convention: a

Above: The brightly illuminated Opera House as seen from the ditch in front of the city walls.
Right: The Human Rights Prize award ceremony in 1995 was held in the Opera House.

Führer loge and Richard Wagner's Meistersingers.

What remains of Hitler's building mania lies between the fairgrounds and Dutzendteich Pond. Tourists are amazed by the crumbling white shell limestone steps with the red brick base showing through. Here is the Zeppelin Tribunal of the Third Reich that was to last 1,000 years; this is where massive party rallies were held. Albert Speer's architectural creations didn't even last a half century and in the meantime, large holes have been filled in with concrete. From the steep steps of the tribunal leading up to the former Führer

Upper left corner: The Nazi Party Rally Grounds Documentation Center penetrates the walls of the Congress Center designed by Albert Speer.

Above: The Zeppelin tribunal on the parade field grounds had a capacity of 70,000 spectators. Nowadays these grounds are used to hold open air concerts and car races.

Right: The victorious Allied Powers used Courtroom 600 as the venue for the Nuremberg Trials.

Following pages: The Dutzendteich Pond attracts city dwellers looking for recreation. The Congress Center in the background is modeled after the Coliseum in Rome.

podium, the 300-square meter parade field comes into view. During the party rallies between 1933 and 1938, up to a quarter of a million people marched here, carried out military exercises and performed Germanic customs such as throwing tree trunks. The tribunal was built to resemble the ancient Greek Pergamon altar. The Congress Center which resembled a larger version of the Coliseum in Rome remained a torso on the shores of the Dutzendteich Pond. The foundations for the German Stadium were dug but the stadium was never completed.

Hitler saw a definite link between his party rallies and the medieval title of "City of Imperial Diets." The National Socialist party made good use of the romanticizion of the former Imperial City of 17th century. Nineteenth century poets such as Wilhelm Wackenroder had nostalgically brought Nuremberg back to life by swarming over the "former world-renowned city" with its "crooked, narrow lanes" and "ancestral buildings and churches in which lasting impressions of our forefathers remain." The Nazis had the city walls repaired, restored old half-timbered buildings to their former glory, turned the Imperial stables at the Fortress into a youth hostel, reintroduced

the Christkindl Market and had the Imperial Jewels brought back from Vienna.

Nuremberg was also attractive because it was a rail hub and had sufficient, flat open land nearby. Moreover, since 1933 the party could rely on a willing and sympathizing police force and system of justice. Since the twenties, Julius Streicher, known as the Franconian Führer, had been stirring up anti-Semitic propaganda in a primitive smear sheet called "Der Stürmer." Nine thousand Jews resided in Nuremberg at the beginning of Hitler's takeover: they were reasonably wealthy, integrated and committed members of the community. At the war's end, a mere 40 Jews were living in hiding in Nuremberg. The city of Nuremberg is where, in 1935, the Nuremberg Laws were laid down in which Jews were denigrated to second class citizens and forbidden to associate with members of the Aryan race. After the war, the victorious Allied Powers tried Nazi war criminals here during the Nuremberg Trials.

A light, angular construction of concrete and glass stands in sharp contrast to the monumental round sandstone arch of the Coliseum. This building serves as a museum and education center for young and old alike. The museum's architecture defines a conscientious approach to and handling of the Third Reich. The Nazi Party Grounds Documentation Center in the north wing of the Congress Center describes the causes, connections, and consequences of the National Socialists and their despotism in the permanent collection entitled "Fascination and Violence."

Boats on the Dutzendteich Pond have been rowing past the rear wall of the Zeppelin Tribunal for decades and the Congress Center serves as a backdrop for local Folk Festivals. The true function of such Nazi architecture has long been forgotten. Novice and expert tennis players alike perfect their techniques on the rear tribunal wall and the Zeppelin Parade Grounds are now used to hold open

Left: An aerial view of Dutzendteich Pond and the Coliseum with the Folk Festival Grounds in the background.

air concerts, car races, and inline skating competitions.

The historic courtroom of the Nuremberg Trials located in Fürtherstrasse is a part of this documentation. Nuremberg has come to grips with its grim past and has documented National Socialist megalomania based on its effects on the city's history. The city has also seized upon the crimes against humanity that became evident around the world during the Nuremberg Trials, and it is committed to protecting human rights worldwide.

Once again, a Jewish community is being reestablished. Almost 20% of Nuremberg's inhabitants nowadays come from another country.

Technology buffs should not miss the German Rail Museum and Transportation Museum next to the Opera House. The 170-year history of trains in Germany can be closely scrutinized – everything from a

Top: Clouds gather above Neunhof Castle.

Above: The fortified church in Kraftshof looks out across the cultivated fields of Garlic Country.

Right: A copy of Neptune Fountain, originally designed for the Market Place, now stands in the City Park.

copy of Germany's first train, the Adler, which ran between Fürth and Nuremberg as of 1835, to the modern ICE 3 locomotive of the 21st century. East of the Old Town is the equally interesting Museum for Industrial Culture in Nuremberg where both the industrial and social-historical story of Nuremberg can be perused.

Fortified Churches and Garlic Country

A visit to the environs north of Nuremberg passes through the City Park and leads to a few Franconian villages in Garlic Country, the vegetable gardens of the city's inhabitants. The village church in Kraftshof is one of the most charming fortified churches in Franconia and its parapets are accessible in part. Although other villages in the region were incorporated into the metropolis in 1972, these farming hamlets have maintained their centers and imperial stately homes. Almoshof once had four such buildings, only one of which, the Holzschuher Castle with its park grounds, still exists. The Franconian stonework in the park reminds one of the Hesperidian Gardens in Johannis. The fact

that Neunhof Castle with its outbuildings and Baroque gardens was once moated can still be discerned. The small museum on the premises offers an overview of patrician life in the country. Hallersche Castle is in Großgründlach; it was erected on the foundation of medieval fortifications and dates back to 1695.

The inhabitants of Nuremberg share a special affinity for their Garlic Country since it has been supplying them with fresh produce for over 500 years. It is not unusual to find exotic types of lettuce and organic tomatoes and zucchini grown in Franconia at the local markets. Family owned and operated greenhouses provide fresh vegetables throughout the year and offer the locovore a healthy alternative to supermarket products. Garlic Country has become a synonym for the intact countryside outside the city walls where walkers and cyclists alike can see and smell fields of thriving produce. Everyone knows the local farmers who use fertilizers sparingly or not at all. This green zone does more than merely preserve a 1000-year old cultural landscape of quaint villages and monuments; more importantly, it keeps industrial parks at bay.

Examining Nuremberg's rich, historical past helps the visitor better understand the complexity of the city today. The once traditional electric and electronics industries as well as transportation services have made room for services and communications industries. New companies and cultural centers are opening their doors where former industries thrived. The city welcomes the visitor to take a stroll through Nuremberg's history and rediscover the medieval, narrow lanes flanked by quaint half-timbered buildings and elegant patrician edifices. The changes that industrialization manifested and the horrors of the Führer are also open to examination. And, not to be forgotten, Nuremberg looks proudly to the future as an important European metropolis, a city of economic growth committed to human rights and as a cosmopolitan home offering quality of life to its inhabitants.

Above: Seen from the ditches north of the fortress, night falls on the Kaiserburg.